Introduction

Bristol Rovers is a unique club in so many ways and, as far as we are aware, is the first football club to feature a poem about 'the beautiful game' in each matchday programme.

Now some of these poems have been collated into this little book and, ever aware of those less fortunate, Rovers are delighted to support the Children's Hospice South West with this publication.

Best *Wishes*

Credits

When Dr Scumbrum's education reached sport and football, he immediately gravitated towards the Blue side of Bristol.

He has supported Bristol Rovers since before the days when he used to put the half time scores up at the Muller Road end on the A B & C boards! He now largely spends his time between working, bubbling away inventing new packaging and writing a novel. He also has a habit of waking up early, inspired into poetry by his beloved Rovers. Driven to help Rovers and the Children's Hospice South West, his hope is that you will tell all your friends to buy their own copy of this book rather than read yours!

Keith Brookman has worked hard to bring this project to fruition and has edited this, hopefully, first volume of Rovers related poems. He has been ably assisted by Ann Walter, who designed and produced the layout, with photographs by JMP UK.

Thanks also, to Kerry Price for her invaluable help, and to all of our advertisers.

This little book is dedicated to Sid and Lil. They both loved Rovers and Sid also liked penning humorous poetry, so I guess we have to blame him...

Supporting
children's hospice
SOUTH WEST
Registered Charity No. 1003314

Dr Scumbrum

1

The World has Changed

My childhood was quite uneventful, compared to so many others,
Though I knew when I was growing up, that I'd once had an older Brother,
I never did get to meet him, I only glimpsed some old photographs,
Him cradled in my Mother's arms, a smile captured in sepia laughs.

My Brother was just eighteen months, when his short life slipped away,
I would never meet my older Bro, or see him laugh and play,
My parents bore the pain of loss, in silence as so many do,
They didn't speak of their Tony much, but their love always held true.

This was 1946, when the world had just been saved,
And my parents still in uniform, could afford no fancy grave,
No headstone for my Brother then, just some flowers to mark the plot,
Only years later we did honour him, with a plaque to mark his spot.

That was a long time ago and the world has, thankfully, moved on.

The illness that took my little brother might have been cured now. Time and progress move hand in hand. The wonder of medical science today is that it is constantly moving forward, always progressing. So yesterday's tragedy can be today's cure, and every new day brings new hope.

But when current knowledge runs out and we are at a loss to answer a family tragedy, the fact that we have such a caring and wonderful place as the Children's Hospice South West is a blessing to be celebrated.

Bristol Rovers understand their small place in society. They try to lift the spirits of their supporters and of our community. Being part of this community is important to Rovers, but we stand humbled by the great work of the Children's Hospice South West, and are delighted to support their cause through this publication as well as in other ways. The Hospice does such great work. Where tears fall, they comfort. Where there is comfort, there is hope, and where there is hope, there is a future.

Dr Scumbrum

Journey to the Centre Spot...

GPS is very accurate, to within an inch or two they say,
So I decided to wear my techno head and play around one day,
I set myself a target, and I gave it all I got,
To work out where in IKEA, was old Eastville's centre spot.

I worked out the grid references, and longitude and lat',
And by jove I went and found it, well I'll eat my bloomin' hat!
I set off for IKEA, with my satnav tuned in and pinging,
And as I went up the big stairs inside, I was sure 'Irene' was singing.

The centre spot was honing in, so I knew where I was heading,
And as I wandered through it left and right, I found myself in bedding,
Just before a large divan my satnav said "You're Here",
But when I set my football down, things started to go queer.

The ball acted like a switch it seemed, for when I placed it down,
Just like a scene from 'Dr Who', all around me span around,
A swirling mist surrounded me and through the fog the Tote End rose,
And the ghosts of a thousand Greyhounds, ran right past my nose.

As the mists and clouds then faded, the floodlights all came on,
I could see the stands were bursting full, and IKEA had simply gone,
Like nectar from old heavens past, a scent then filled the air,
As the gasworks released its familiar smell, ah, then I knew that I was there.

It all seemed in slow motion, as I stood there on the pitch,
I felt just like a millionaire, I had never felt so rich,
The teams appeared before me, and the crowd gave out a roar,
And as the quartered shirts came running out, my heart began to soar.

Just like it was magic, I stood there in a trance,
As Harold thundered down the wing, and beat three defenders in a dance,
He crossed the ball for Alfie Biggs, who walloped in a shot,
That flew right past their goalkeeper, and the crowd liked that a lot.

But the celebrations faded, as the mists swirled around again,
The scene before me disappeared, and my head then reeled in pain,
I came too again in IKEA, but could tell no one at all,
Then what upset me most of all, was that some sod had nicked my ball!

To the unititiated, Eastville was the home of Bristol Rovers from
1897 until 1996. The site is now home to a IKEA store.

Photo: Tom Lockyer celebrates at Wembley

The Rovers Return...

Farewell to the Conference, adios my friends, goodbye,
You'll understand that we have to go, but please don't fret or cry,
We know you'll miss our travelling fans and record gate receipts,
It's sure been an experience, but one we hope not to repeat.

No more trips to Braintree, Alfreton or Dover,
No more coach to Gateshead, for the 12th Man travelling Rover,
We won the right at Wembley, to rise to higher things,
With hope that our ambitions will finally now grow wings.

We leave behind some proud old teams and names with history,
Why they languish where they are, is just a mystery,
Poor souls like good old Grimsby, Wrexham and Torquay,
We wish them well and all the best, but now we have to flee.

The Football League awaits us, but listen up for sure,
Now we've tasted sweet success, we're hungry for some more,
The Pirate flame is burning fierce, we are not here just for fun,
Sing 'Irene' long and loud my friends, as we target League One!

Sound the horn and lead the charge, till death us now do part,
For once again we have a team that plays with skill and heart,
With Bournemouth an example; and Darrell at the wheel,
Double Bubble promotions could be ours for real...

When Rovers gained promotion from the Football Conference.
It turned out to be a predictive poem!

Photo: Phil Kite

An Ode to Phil Kite, Living Legend and Gentleman

I've been listing Rovers heroes, and try hard as I might,
I can't think of many out there, to match our own Phil Kite,
A man of many talents, and dedicated to a fault,
Let's start with the green jersey, and the crosses that he caught.

Phil the kid was mighty, a colossus of a lad,
Who discovered that between the sticks, he wasn't all too bad,
He could fly right through the air, like a kite held in a breeze,
And tip a ball around the post, with the greatest of ease.

England came a calling and he wore Three Lions as a boy,
Presents for Phil were easy then, just gloves and no fancy toy,
Fearless then as always, he would dive at any forwards feet,
And when signing on for Rovers, he joined Bristol's elite.

He quickly impressed the manager, who picked him for the team,
Fulfilling then for Kitey, an early childhood dream,
Our Phil was most impressive, and drew the watchful eye,
Of scouts from the very Saints themselves, who wanted this kite to fly.

His career then grew and blossomed, and he raised many a cheer,
Gracing some great football teams, for sixteen solid years,
We forgive him now his last club, though it was a blooming pity,
That he ended up across the road, at a certain Bristol City!
(We all have bills to pay)!

But the call of his heart was too strong, and he came back to The Gas,
With the chance to be our physio, being just too good to pass,
His abilities with the magic sponge, were made to all quite clear,
And over his time he became a rock, as his stay spanned 36 years.

How many men has he treated? How many careers has he saved?
Modest Phil wouldn't tell you, he's not one to boast or to rave,
But injuries tend not to take days off, so Phil hasn't had time to rest,
And in the league table of heroes, Kitey's up there with the best.

So the time has come to salute you, and once again let this Kite fly,
But think of this man as you next sing, "I'm Rovers till I die",
He typifies what this club is about, and best wishes we'd all like to send,
For Phil Kite is surely a legend, and a Gashead right through to the end.

Ship Shape and Bristol Fashion

One rarely hears the saying now, 'Ship Shape and Bristol Fashion',
Not least or in any ways, said with any pride or passion,
The old saying means that things are grand, and all is at its best,
Only Bristol has such a reference, our lovely Bristol, here in the West.

In olden days, a Rover sailed the oceans, and roamed the seven seas,
So think then of our emblem, a Pirate proud and pleased,
It seems to have been our destiny, to have wandered in the past,
From Eastville out to Twerton, then back to Bristol again at last.

The oldest club in Bristol, the only one that spans long years, (we can beat 1982 Ltd),
We're used to doing things the hard way, and discarding the odd tear,
All the plans we've had in the past, to build ourselves a home,
Have been wrecked by our opponents, who want us just to roam.

But 'steady as she goes' my friends, keep a firm hand on the tiller,
Trust in Captain Higgs and his crew, to sail us through this courtroom thriller,
From the high seas to the high court, we'll battle barristers and waves,
Until our new home has a harbour, and our very club is saved.

Ship shape and Bristol fashion boys, remember that good and right,
Will come to those that don't give up, and carry on the fight,
So get behind the team today, and shout out long and loud,
For we are Bristol Rovers, and in Bristol fashion, stay true and proud.

*Written as the club started to 'do Battle' in the High Court
over Sainsbury's decision to wriggle out of their contract with Rovers*

There is Superstition

No I'm not superstitious, I don't believe in all that rot,
Though my mate on the terrace, believes in it a lot,
He'll wear the same shirt every week, but only if we win,
But like my patience after time, his shirt is wearing thin.

It's only that this shirt of his, (it didn't cost him that much dosh),
But his superstition is that if we win, it won't get a wash,
So when we're on a winning streak, he never stops to think,
He's standing there with his arms aloft, causing quite a stink!

His superstition tells him, that on matchdays he's to take,
The same route every Saturday, whatever roadworks they make,
And walking on the pavement, he'll sometime step right back,
'Cos the one thing that he mustn't do, is step on any crack.

He wouldn't have his hair cut, so long as they didn't lose away,
So after Leyton Orient, his long suffering wife gave a loud 'Hurray'
The shearing was like a ceremony, and the barber charged no fee,
'Cos they gathered up a sack of it, and made loads for charity.

He tells me he's got underpants, that have winning mystic powers,
So last year in The Conference, they stayed on for bloody hours,
He started walking funny, so stiff that he couldn't march,
Like his jeans they had been treated, with double Robin starch.

He'd waddle up to the turnstile, like he had his own force field,
The queue would smell him coming, and the crowd would quickly yield,
I love this club I really do, and I savour every win,
But at one point I had wished we'd lose, so his pants would hit the bin!

No I'm not superstitious, I don't believe in all of that,
Now where's my special Rovers top, and my lucky hat...

Sundays...

I love a Sunday morning when we've won,
Even waking in the rain, the world seems full of sun,
The fog of waking disappears and a smile begins to beam,
As yesterday's sweet victory, is remembered as no dream.

I watch the footy highlights, with an early cup of tea,
Replaying all the Rovers goals, as I savour victory,
A glance at the league table, soon brings a rapid smile,
Ah, it's such a lovely feeling, I hope it lasts a while...

I hate a Sunday morning when we lost the day before,
The morning sun seems watery, and the bird song is a bore,
My Sunday jobs seem endless, and just too much to do,
And I spend the day lethargic, feeling sad and blue.

But when we've won, Sunday's jobs get done, in such a jolly way,
All tasks complete, seemed no mean feat, as I whistle through the day,
I tell my wife she's beautiful, and offer to take her shopping,
Though my whistle starts to peter out, when I start bloomin' dropping!
  (Is it just me? I have lots of energy... until it comes to shopping
  which seems to drain me more than giving three pints of blood, all at once!
Sorry, I digress, back to the twaddle)...

Saturday has come again, and I'm off now to the Mem,
Full of anticipation, for a good result again,
And then I found my wife in prayer, and thought she'd committed a sin,
No she said, rising from the floor, I just hope they bloody win!

Cup Fever...

Once upon a time ago, I played a prelim round,
I dreamt of reaching Wembley, of being discovered (or just found!),
Of course I didn't make it, but still I had that dream,
As every young lad does today, of playing for their team.

I was asked to be the sweeper, a role I'd played before,
A piece of cake for a centre half so nothing to endure,
Then the boss said "ah now don't get changed, just stay here in the room",
I was confused until he grinned aloud, and handed me a broom!

There's something about the FA Cup, it's unique in every way,
Where else can one see great minnows, proudly have their day?
All year round they train for this, with strict diets for their belly,
Just to have a day like this, and to make in on the telly!

So today I woke up in a sweat, but then I am a believer,
It's first round day and yes you guessed, I've got FA Cup fever,
Once again the dream will start, for all teams big and small,
From Arsenal down to Accrington, it's still the same round ball.

Welcome to Chesham and your fans, we know it's a big day,
We'll do our best to entertain and see that there's fair play,
And welcome back a legend, we salute you Barry Hayles,
You'll no doubt see the quartered shirt, and recall lots of tales.

And while we wish Baz all the best, he'll understand for sure,
It can't extend to this particular game, though he might wish for more,
We'd love to have a cup run, for fans, for club and team,
And show the world the quartered shirts and live our own cup dream.

So sing up Gas and sing up loud, let's make a decent sound,
I think we're on the telly, and it's target second round!

Bless them. Chesham were the Cup shock of the day and helped us focus on the league!

A Message to The Team

Halloween came recently amid a mighty storm,
And as the lightning crackled, I thought of our home form,
Grim shadows in the darkness, were lit between the thunder,
As flashes then of recent games, appeared in ghostly wonder.

I tried to hide my eyes in fear, as the Newport game appeared,
Accrington and Oxford came, in the flashes all so weird,
I had not believed in demons then, and I prayed they'd go away,
All darkened then my Halloween, and I hoped they would not stay.

How strange I thought this team of ours, so magnificent away,
Yet come back to The Mem, and then the demons come to play,
It might be psychological, that despairing phantoms come,
Or was it just some recent curse, leaving us so numb?

But no...

This team of ours so brave away, need fear no team down here,
So cast aside your doubts brave boys, we're behind you with a cheer
The only demons that you really have, are the ones you keep inside,
And they will be sent packing lads, if you play with steel and pride.

The crowd are all behind you, your only fear is fear itself,
So cast that off behind you boys, and the win will bring its wealth,
Carlisle come here on Saturday, and the past is in the bin,
So confidence and trust now boys, we know that you can win.

Past games are now just history, and today we start anew,
Time to caste off demons boys, and trust in the quarters blue.

*Written after the start to the 2015/16 season when we won
many more games away than at home!*

Our Stuart

Stuart Sinclair is a Rover, who stands out on the field,
He's nine feet tall in the tackle, and I've never seen him yield,
A terrier or Rottweiler, who'll never give up the chase,
And who despite only having little legs, has never lacked for pace.

I've watched this team for many years, and seen players come and go,
But rarely as with our Stuart, does the spirit so loudly show,
He typifies what we want to see, and I've never been irate,
Watching Stuart run around, he even looks like a Pirate!

If you were in the trenches, you'd want him by your side,
And when the ball is at his feet, he fills us all with pride,
His engine is fixed on overdrive, and I've never seen him tire,
And what endears him most of all, is that he is such a trier.

Stuart's history is itself a tale, and a story to make one wonder,
Of how he missed the league before, is surely a scouting blunder,
Not short of skill nor football guile, he might never have made his mark,
Had it not been for the scouting skills, of our very own Darrell Clarke

Stuart is a true Gas name, with some great ones in the past,
For instance Stuart Taylor, who nailed a record to the mast,
   (that will never be broken by the way)
Never will there ever be, such loyalty to our club,
546 appearances, even more if you count him as sub.

And then there's Stuart Campbell, who stood out loud and clear,
As being one who clearly held, the quartered shirt so dear,
Just as with Stuart Sinclair, he typified what's best,
The passion and the effort, made him stand out from the rest.

So we salute you Stuart Sinclair, and await today's rendition,
Of showing us what's best in class, in the very best Gas tradition,
Keep doing what you're doing lad, and wear that shirt with pride,
Because we know that when the chips are down, you're never one to hide.

I Wish...

I wish I was a director, of my beloved football club,
But I ain't got no money, and therein lies the rub,
I'd love to win the lottery, and scoop that Euro cash,
I'd be straight down to Mr Higgs, with my cheque book at a dash.

I'd show Nick my Gas tattoo, stencilled on me leg,
And hope he'd let me join the board, and that I wouldn't have to beg,
I know that he would have to know, that I truly loved The Gas,
So I'd show him my Pirate tattoo, emblazoned across my … arm!

I'd sit there with a big cigar, lording it with me betters,
And write out cheques for this and that, ignoring begging letters,
The fans would sing my name out loud, as long as we were winning,
Ahh yes, I can see it now, a Gastastic new beginning.

I'd go and buy that Gareth Bale, Lambert and a few,
The team photo would be a picture, in their quartered blue,
We'd build a gurt big stadium, for sixty thou' or more,
It would be the Wembley of the West, and you'd pay to have a tour.

Then one day my bank manager, would ring me with a shout,
"I'm sorry to have to tell you, but yer money's running out",
"You'll have to make some cut backs, no more to the boys in blue,"
And the team would slump in The Premiership, down to number two!

Supporters would start shouting, that they thought that I should go,
And boo me as I took my seat, if only they did know,
I thought they loved me 'cos I'm me, isn't life so funny,
It seemed that somehow after all, they only loved me for my money.

I wish I was a director, of my beloved football team,
But then again, perhaps after all, it is best just to dream...

Written long before Wael beat me to the job!

We Three Kings...

Seasons Greetings to our visitors, welcome to the Or-i-ent,
And thank you for your three Kings, for they were heaven sent,
We'd be pleased if you remember, that it's the time of year for gifts,
And that three points coming our way, would sure give us a lift!
(Well I did send a letter to Santa)

And welcome all Ye Gasheads, each one of you a Gem,
It's just like coming home again, when we arrive back at the Mem,
Christmas came and Christmas went, with lots of festive cheer,
With so much over indulgence, I couldn't face another beer!
(Well, go on then, just the one...)

Too much cake and Turkey, I nearly ate the house,
But now my diets kicking in, and I'm eating like a mouse,
So I'll only have two pasties now, well, they are 'Memorially' good,
Then I'll go back again to abstinence, as I know I really should.

And spare a thought for the lads out there, whose Christmas is on hold,
No turkey blowouts for the boys in blue, just training in the cold,
You'll see their dedication now, designed to make you merry,
And perhaps then if we can take three points, they can have a tiny sherry!

Who would be a footballer, (or anyone around the club), with a fixture list so tough,
So while we welcome this festive time, for them it must be rough,
Luton follow Orient, straight after the Dons and Daggers,
Cheers to the guys that wrote the fixture list, and the other carpet baggers.

We'll hope see you all next year, with Luton here next week,
And we'll go all out for the double then, for that is what we'll seek,
Let's hope that twenty sixteen, will bring us all a smile,
We can surely trust that Darrell and the Boys, will go the extra mile.

A Merry Christmas 2015 message from Dr S.

Welcome to the New Year...

Well what a New Year that was, so much for the idyllic dream,
I've just eaten the last bit of turkey, and slightly off whipped cream,
My guts have all but exploded, and my belt don't fit any more,
After all those days of 'festive fun', it was becoming quite a bore.

The first row broke out Christmas Eve, when I cut the carrots wrong,
And I started swearing loudly, when someone sang that song,
    (something about a seasonal bird with a red breast bob bob bobbin along!)
The next row came as I'd not taken, the turkey out the freezer,
And my joke with pepper in the crackers, turned into a sneezer!
    (That were a good un that, added some 'seasoning' to the festive season!)

I received a pair of socks and scarf, in exchange for an expensive ring,
So sitting around the tree in my scarf, I didn't want to sing,
If it's better to give than to receive, then I've had a cracking time,
(Whatever smart arse dreamt that up, found an alternative to crime!)

Word went out that I'd a beer barrel, chilling by the cellar wall,
And then strangely out of nowhere, lots of 'old friends' came to call,
Folks appeared I ain't seen for years, and then only knew by and by,
But like locusts they descended, and drank my barrel dry!

The longer it all dragged on, the more I dreamt again,
Of getting back to normality, and being back at The Mem,
I've done with all that tinsel, and repeats on the telly,
And stuffing everything I could eat, down me blooming belly.

So a "Happy New Year" everyone, welcome back to The Mem,
It's time to get the football out and cheer on the boys again,
While we've all been pigging out, with belts all tight and straining,
They poor lads have been training hard, even when it's raining.

Luton Town are here today, and very welcome so they are,
It's a fair old distance down here, by coach or in a car,
We hope their season goes well, though they'll understand it when I say,
They are welcome to take points anytime, except that is today!

A Happy New Year message 2016

I Rest My Case...

I dreamt a dream one darkened night, when the moon did not appear,
A court scene lay before my eyes, and it all seemed real and near,
I sat between the gowns and wigs, my head confused and reeling,
I had been here before you see, so sat here quietly appealing!

I was there as the victim, in a fight t'ween right and wrong,
The guilty party glared right back and the case was taking long,
My innocence for all to see, was written on my face,
Though the accused were acting innocent, and my heart began to race.

I put my faith in the judiciary, and that truth and right would win,
I had been badly wronged you see, and in truth there is no sin,
But the other side were scheming hard, and as tricky as could be,
With twists and turns they blurred the truth, and it would be hard for me.

They'd wanted to buy land from me, and promised that in writing,
But as their fortunes waned in time, they reneged and came out fighting,
Their words it seems were cunning, and written in such a way,
That even though 'twas morally wrong, they could swear that night was day.

And in my dream I listened hard, as the story did unfold,
It seemed they were well versed in tricks, and the plot well used of old,
I was clearly not the first you see, to suffer in such a way,
To them it was a practiced game, and just another day.

Their lawyers sat in long black gowns and I wondered in a fright,
If by day they drew their darkest plans, and drank human blood at night,
That dreadful thought then wakened me, and my dream was gone for good,
I would never know if I won my case, as my world knew that I should.

It seems there is a difference now, between moral and legal right,
That even though you've been badly wronged, for truth one has to fight,
The moral of the story is, that some people just don't have morals,
They'll bully you and hope their size, will put you off the quarrel.

Some people may dread nightmares, and monsters they can hate,
But in truth most monsters now wear suits, and are often corporate,
A bad man carries knives and guns, but the most dangerous of men,
Doesn't need a gun at all... but just more ink to fill his pen.

Written as we awaited the Sainsbury's Court Appeal…

GASHEAD NETWORK
Official Business Network of Bristol Rovers FC

We are a network of business owners working in conjunction with Bristol Rovers FC, we hold our network meetings at the Memorial Stadium.

Our members benefit from monthly meetings and direct business promotion to the fan base via our social media channels, with over 1000 subscribers.

www.gasheadnetwork.co.uk
enquiries: contact@brand14.com

The Beautiful Game

I learnt so much from football, when I was growing as a boy,
And my dubbined leather lace up ball, was by far my favourite toy,
Football taught me right from wrong and how no one liked a cheat,
That it was better to lose than take a dive, and not to moan or bleat.

I learnt that hard work gave its reward and, to be persistent,
And that just as in life itself, one needs to be consistent,
I learnt to lose with dignity, (did that a lot unfortunately!) and to win with modesty,
And that teamwork made for winning, and that would do for me.

So when I read of FIFA, as the mud begins to stick,
I think of how our game's been robbed, and it really makes me sick,
I hear about the FBI, and the corruption at football's top,
And my blood begins to really boil, and demand that it must stop.

I read that kids in poorer countries, didn't get a football pitch
Because the likes of Jack Warner, stole the money to get rich,
So the poorest kids just went without, while Sepp Blatter took his fee,
Robbing not just the third world, but the likes of you and me.

The game's been run by parasites, and we need to drive them out,
At the very top of football, there needs to be a rout,
There is no place for dirty deals, on TV or ticket money,
And the World Cup in the desert? Well, we all knew that deal was 'funny'.

I even feel the English game, has lost some moral standing,
When the agents of Premiership players, stand there just demanding,
Once again your money goes, just to feed a greedy few,
And we stand here and accept it, like there's nothing we can do.

But just like you I love this game and I simply want it back,
I want to throw corruption out, and get football back on track,
It truly is 'the beautiful game', where one can hope and dream,
And I still aspire for that today, with winning hopes for our team.

This for me is what it's truly about, simple effort and endeavour,
Just show me 22 lads that try, and it's still the best game ever,
We may not be a rich club and in some ways it doesn't matter,
And I would certainly trust our own Nick Higgs, rather than one Sepp Blatter!

Sure, Premiership Football's very good, but some parts need a fix,
And for proof, the last time England won anything... was in nineteen sixty six!
And that my friends, was almost exactly 50 years ago!

Written after yet another FIFA storm

Irene and The Gas...

Friends of mine from out of town see me in a different light,
When they hear me whistle happily, our song 'Irene Goodnight',
A confused smile spreads across their face, when I relate the tale,
Of how 'Irene' became Rovers song, and I'm smiling without fail.

"We've been singing it since the fifties", I tell them very proudly,
"And there's nothing out there like it, when The Gas sing 'Irene' loudly",
I tell them of old 'Lead Belly', an intriguing tale for sure,
Of how he sung himself from the gallows, with Irene's lament so pure.*

Now part of Rovers history, when it started back at Eastville,
The Plymouth fans all taunted us, but t'was grist to Rovers mill,
We started singing 'Irene', and then it seemed to stick,
Especially when we found out, that it got on City's wick!

'Cos when other teams insult us, we tend to turn it round,
The City thought that Gasheads, would upset us but they found,
That we rose above the insult, and grabbed it to our heart,
And like so much from the Red side, it's all hot air and …wind!

So 'Irene Goodnight' became 'our song,' and I never fail to smile,
When The Gas are out in full voice, it's the best song by a mile,
The opposition stand there, with faces confused and in shock,
As 'Irene' rings out around them, and the Gasheads make it rock.

When my Mum and Dad both passed away, 'Irene' was their last song,
It's soft lament so melodically, played their lives out good and long,
'Irene' drifted through the headstones, as we said a sad farewell,
And one day it will see me off, but when that is I can't tell!

Their spirit lives on and is here today, I can hear them in that song,
So sing up Gasheads, sing 'Irene', and sing it loud and long,
Be proud that we are different, and have Irene in our tradition,
Go on Gas, sing it again, give it your best rendition...

If you don't know the story of 'Huddy' Ledbetter, then listen up. Convicted of murder and awaiting hanging, 'Lead Belly' as he was known, received a pardon when the Governor of the Texas prison heard him singing 'Irene'. It touched his heart, as it does ours... He not only received a pardon but was released to later take up a recording contract. Lead Belly became the King of the 12 string guitar and an early sole legend. Hollywood should make a film of his life story as true stories are sometimes better than fiction...

History Full Circle

Back in 1883 football was unexplored and new,
This was long before the quartered shirts, in good old white and blue,
Sport then was very different, with 'Chariots of Fire' style racers,
And rugby boys in baggy shorts, all mustachio'd egg chasers!

The Black Arabs were a local team, who chased the odd shaped ball,
Until some of these fine rugby lads, heard a different sporting call,
They thought that this new round ball game, might bring them lots of fun,
So they forming a brand new football team, in the bright September sun.

'Twas the birth of Bristol Rovers, and the Black Arabs trailed the way,
They formed Bristol's first football team, and the Rovers we know today,
They played in black with a yellow sash and did their very best,
To make a family friendly club, and the best team in the West.

The Black Arabs knew just what to do, and soon forged a reputation,
That over time grew enough in size, to impress the entire nation.
The 'Black Arabs' changed to 'Bristol Rovers', now this would be a hit,
And the transformation was then completed, with a unique quartered kit.

Soon the crowds were queuing, to see the boys in blue,
Land at Eastville was then acquired and a stadium built sparkling new,
Years came and went and over time, Rovers fortunes just like the tide,
Ebbed and flowed with success and less, but then never lost their pride.

Eastville was sold and went to the dogs, as our fortunes waned and dipped,
But the spirit lived on proud and strong, as out to Trumpton we were shipped,
Good old Denis Dunford, steered the ship through rough sea's again,
And the rugby boys then played a part, as we were invited to the Mem.

Nick Higgs and co then took control, and set out the task ahead,
To run a tight ship for this club, and from the very front they led,
The foundations of the club were strong, and its supporters the very best,
No boom and bust like the lot in red, for the Rovers were above the rest.

And then from the land of Jordan, a white light was seen to glow,
From the Hashemite Kingdom proud and true, a new Gashead seemed to know,
That in finding Bristol Rovers, he had found a sleeping giant,
Who had waited in the wings too long, and to adversity had been defiant.

He looked upon this fine club of ours, and saw both history and potential,
With a sprinkling of fine Byzantine dust, future glory could be exponential,
So here we are once more today, watching history unfold,
Full circle from the black to white, as a new story will be told.

I'm sure those old Black Arab boys would smile now looking down,
As Wael and the family, now take up their proudest crown,
It's clear that with Bristol Rovers, one important and clear facet,
Is that it's the fans who've spanned the years, that are in fact, their biggest asset...

Written after Wael arrived

Lest We Forget...

The tears of one's own Grandmother were oh so hard to endure,
Each sweet droplet pained in anguish, each sweet tear so clear and pure,
I watched my grandma say goodbye to the one man of her life,
They had seen two wars together, and enjoyed long years as man and wife.

Grandfather was a quiet man who had fought the First World War,
The experience left the deepest scars that had changed him to the core,
His medals, like his mental scars, were hidden deeply out of sight,
But he returned to marry his sweetheart and raise a family straight and right.

His son, my father, also heard the call to go to war,
Like so many of his time before, he played a part in Hitler's fall,
Like his father did before him, he returned to live his life,
Doing his best for everyone, for his family and his loving wife.

Wars are men making madness when our leaders are out for a fight,
They then ask us millions to join them, swearing by God that it's right,
Foreign fields laying silent with the graves of our boys in neat rows of poppies so red,
The right and wrongs we don't question here, but it is right to remember our dead.

It's right to remember the fallen, though no one condones why they fell,
It's right to remember those brave boys whose lives so often ended in hell,
So, on every November eleven, it's so right to put two minutes aside,
To stand in silence and remember, wearing poppies with honour and pride.

So when football's international body bans Great Britain from showing respect,
It's they who should take time to consider, take time to deeply reflect,
For the free world is free for one reason, a reason that should never be lost,
The price of that freedom was our brave boys' lives, surely the ultimate cost.

So while FIFA sit in luxury in Zurich, enjoying the good life that they all now lead,
They disrespect our British way now, to remember those who even still bleed,
FIFA should now reconsider and let poppies grow before it's too late,
For I still remember my grandma, and know why the word before Britain is Great!

Do not forget, for to remember and reflect is the
best way of avoiding the madness of another war.

The Rovers Rollercoaster...

Following Bristol Rovers, is like a parody of life,
We ride some highs of great joy, but the next day is filled with strife,
We've learned to ride the ups and downs, as only Rovers can,
Like my old Dad told me many times, "it's the setbacks that will make you a man".

Well even the youngest Rovers fans, have learned to grow up pretty fast,
And when we dropped out of the league, some said we wouldn't last,
The rollercoaster was riding hard, and we clung on through the bends,
Wondering if those despairing times, would ever see an end.

The Conference came and off we set, with Darrell at the helm,
The season started pretty slow, like we wouldn't overwhelm,
But we stayed on track and got up speed, to see us finish strong,
And Wembley saw us climb that hill, with the Gasheads in full song.

The rollercoaster kicked in once more, and we off we rode again,
In a month we've seen Wael's big smile, and then encountered courtroom pain,
It sums up Rovers in a line, to have such high hopes then be dashed,
As our less than perfect legal system, is for us now morally trashed.

So down we plunge once more again, with our old plans in the air,
Proving that lawyers and a moral right, don't make a happy pair,
We then rode the rollercoaster, down to Newport's sandy plot,
And all the lads did us so proud, as we climb up to reach third spot.

It's never been an easy road, following our lovely team,
Many's the times our biggest hopes, have failed to meet our dream,
But we ride the setbacks every time, and pick ourselves up again,
And wipe the dust off with a smile, and get back on the train.

We've lived for generations now, as the poor relations here,
As our cousins from across the city, tried to make it clear,
That they thought they had the right divine, to be the biggest club,
Though in truth they've never made it big, so there in lies their rub!

I feel that all around us now, momentum is on our side,
Darrell's finally built a team, that plays with heart and pride,
Yes there will be ups and downs, and no doubt we'll have some pain,
But the rollercoasters now heading up, to the good times once again.

And as to my own shopping habits since JS renaged?

The day that Sainsbury's money died, a lesser club might have laid down and cried,
But we are Bristol Rovers Sir, and to give up the fight did not occur.

Now you don't have to, but I can, give that shop a lifetime ban,
So while their lawyers play the fiddle, I'll give my business now to .... Someone else!

Written after we lost to the Sainsbury's appeal…

The Long and Winding Road...

Not one of us can ever change, in which area we were born,
So I discovered when I was very young, that I was the subject of some scorn,
For my Mum and Dad followed Rovers, as did my Grandfather too,
And swept up on their love of the Gas, I naturally stayed true blue.

The only little problem was, that my part of town was red,
Hence my prowess in athletics, grew from not wishing to be dead!
With the playground gangs of bullies, my blue and white was not a hit,
And my childhood passion for The Gas, certainly made me fit!

So when it came to school sports day, I won every single race,
From sprinting to long distance, no one could match my pace,
With red shirts all around me, it would have been a dreadful sin,
To let anyone wearing a robin motif, go and blooming win!

It's been the same for all of us, and sometimes it's not been funny,
To be the poor relations, to those others 'loads of money',
From Harry Dolman onwards, you can bet yer life my laddie,
That while Rovers had some good honest men, they had a sugar daddy.

We've always been the underdogs, and all suffered some abuse,
Especially when we lost our home, and to Trumpton were cast loose,
'They' always had an attitude, that went with their bigger ground,
And like banging on an empty drum, made a rather hollow sound.

I loved it back in '90, when we beat them to first place,
A hiding dished out at Trumpton, and then Blackpool to win the race,
Twentyman, Yates and Holloway, ah, now that was a classic team,
They epitomised the Rovers, no money or ground, but a dream.

Nowadays we have all grown up, and should learn to get along,
I've many friends in red and white and even though they're wrong,
They are entitled to their opinion, and I respect their point of view,
But I can feel the wind of change is here, and the futures looking 'blue'.

One friend of mine (who'll remain anonymous), made a decision even bolder,
Love conquers all it seems, as he wed a City season ticket holder!
He loves his Sunday's when we win, but true harmony wears thin,
When the Rovers don't do quite so well, and the other lot sneak a win!
(Doesn't happen very often these days...)

Let the bad old days of intolerance, be confined to a distant past,
We all need to 'Kick it Out' and nail our colours to the mast,
The futures looking bright for us and we can hold our heads up high,
With Wael and Steve Hamer at the helm, the limit is now the sky.

So sing up Gasheads, sing long and loud, for what a year it's been,
The seasons drawing to a close and no one could write this scene,
We're up there with the best of them, and although it's nip and tuck,
We've the best team that we've seen for years, we just need... a little luck.

Down To The Wire...

Well here we are with one game to go and wow, it's mighty tight,
There's just three points left to play for, and we're in a real promotion fight,
The dice will roll one last time today, and we'll see which way they fall,
And by Five tonight we will know our fate, but now it's still too close to call.

I'm suddenly a fan of Stevenage, and will be rooting for them today,
And dear old Wycombe? Oh I wish them well, on their local-derby day,
We can only focus on ourselves today, and hope that fate is kind,
Hoping for one last twist in this, a season that has been sublime.

Two years ago we played Mansfield Town, thinking we'd survive,
But the hands of fate dealt us a dreadful blow, and the league cast us aside,
That cruel twist was like an arrow to our hearts, and we endured a summer long,
But today we hope that fate will be kind, and yield a summer bathed in song.

When the season started August time, we simply didn't know,
How much we'd see this team of ours, in skill and stature grow,
Home to old Northampton Town, seems so long now in the past,
And we didn't have the best of starts, but we knew that wouldn't last.

December saw us in the groove, with a draw and four great wins,
A superb way to end the year, that gave us all big Yuletide grins,
Our home form was now in full song, and we were proving hard to beat,
Bristol Rovers were a team it seemed, that no one wanted to meet.

And all this season you supporters, took your loyalty to a new level,
With some of the away trips being a real long distance Devil,
Hartlepool and Morecambe, York and Carlisle too,
Showed that the best supporters, were wearing quartered white and blue.

So whatever happens on this day of days, it certainly must be said,
That there's never been a better time, to be a proud Gashead,
It's going down to the wire for us, and we'll see what dear fate brings,
But it certainly won't be over now, until the old fat lady sings!

And I wonder as the clock winds down, if there might be a twist in the tale,
Last day nerves are a funny thing, so who knows who'll succeed or fail,
If the play offs await us then so it shall be, and we will face those as we see,
Just make sure it's Lee Mansell, who takes the last pen at Wem-bel-lee!

But we can do this today and now it's YOU, that can do your bit today,
Let the boys hear you sing as never before, for it's time to have your say,
Sing long and loud and let everyone, hear you singing for your team,
And if 'Irene' could be heard in Oxford then... with luck we'll fulfill our dream...

Written for the last game of the season against Dagenham & Redbridge…

A Moment In History...

Our fathers used to argue, with their fathers as to who,
Were the greatest Rovers team to wear the white and blue,
They would debate what players, were the finest of their time,
Which era and which manager, had produced a team sublime.

I heard great stories as a child, of old players I didn't know,
In black and white and sepia, their images would grow,
I started watching for myself, and soon I could debate,
What year and players were the best, and of those I chose to rate.

That was a long, long time ago, and many years have now slipped by,
I've watched a thousand Rovers sides, and one or two nearly made me cry!
But what I can say with confidence, is that we're now watching something rare,
An entire squad that play with heart, and you can see how much they care.

Leicester had something similar, you could see how those boys did try,
Against Dagenham we saw that same passion, as the minutes were ticking by,
And as for those ninety minutes, or was it ninety four?
All the excitement of the last game? Well, who could ask for more.
(Apart from my cardiologist!)

Darrell Clarke has built this Rovers team, to a budget and on ration,
To make up for that he has instilled, old fashioned pride and heart and passion,
Take note of what you're watching now, as you're seeing something rare,
A bunch of lads that play for the shirt, and show just how much they care.

I'm so pleased the other Bristol side avoided going down,
'Cos we're climbing fast towards them, and we don't want them to drown,
We'll be with them very, very soon, yes our Bristol Rovers team,
For our time is coming fast my friends, the time to fulfil our dream.

You can cast back in your memories now, to past teams that you have seen,
To the greatest sides and players, that you think have ever been,
And debate amongst your closest friends, because they all will have a view,
But there's one thing beyond question now, it's a concrete fact and true.

If you're aged ten or one hundred, and you've watched this team with me,
Then the last two seasons you have seen, a real piece of history,
For not once in all our proud long years, have we won two promotions side by side,
And in years to come you can say that 'you were there', as you look back again with pride.

And what makes my heart beat faster now, and my imagination to run free?
Is that Darrell has been working hard, on 'Project Promotion - Number Three!'

Written after promotion to League One.

The Dream - Part 1...

I had a dream last night, that I wore the quartered kit,
It must have been a dream, 'cos I could run and I was fit,
I led out the team at Eastville, the crowd was one huge mass,
One of those dreams that was so real, I could even smell the gas.

Harold was out there on the wing, and the Jones trio too,
Ah, it was such a spectacle, all in the white and blue,
The crowd were calling out my name, it made me feel so proud,
And the tannoy system worked a treat, crisp and clear and loud.
(must have been a dream then!)

We were playing Man United, with Charlton and Besty there,
But in my dream we were just as good, and played without a care,
I could thread a pass from 40 yards with absolute precision,
I didn't care a jot for big named teams, I'd just treat em' with derision.

The kick off whistle blew on time and the Tote End gave a roar,
Harold took a pass from me, and down the wing he tore,
In came his cross as always, as perfect as you'd bet,
And I flew through the air majestic, and thumped it in the net.

Number two was easy, a scissor kick precise,
And my hat trick was a free kick, a bender which was nice,
The crowd were chanting "Scumbrum", as I thumped in number four,
It seemed I could run forever, and the crowd they wanted more.

The final whistle went at last and boys, we'd won the cup!
And the Gasheads were in full song, as I went to pick it up,
As I lifted the Cup above my head, my eyes were full of tears,
Then I woke up looking at me wife... I'd lifted her up by her ears!

The Dream - Part 2...

I went straight back to sleep again, and was back in the quartered shirt,
Only this time I was rubbish, and every tackle hurt,
I was playing back at Eastville, I could smell the gas again,
But my shorts were muddy pyjamas, and it had just started to rain.

This dream was bloomin' horrible, so different to before,
I puffed and panted like my Dad, and my passing was so poor,
I was carrying an old banjo, and I could see the cows behind,
But I couldn't hit a darn thing, so the cow it didn't mind.
(Please note that no animals were hurt in the making of this dream)

I moved in a strange slow motion, and my legs just wouldn't run,
This was nothing like my first dream, this was just not any fun,
I looked down at my feet and saw, one slipper and one dap,
And the crowd were shouting "get him off, can't you see he's blooming c**p".

The referee though was very good, so I knew it was a dream,
And I knew I had to wake myself, to flee this horrid scene,
I slapped myself and pinched my arm and stamped on the groundsman's rake,
But I was stuck inside this nightmare, I just couldn't seem to wake.

But then at last it ended, and I was staring at the ceiling,
I had woken and was bathed in sweat, my head was hot and reeling,
My poor old wife was awake too, with a face about to crack,
It seemed I'd be pinching her arm, and thumped her in the back.

So I lay here in the spare bed, with some steak upon my eye,
The last thing that I want is sleep, I don't even want to try,
I might slip back into nightmares, and run round like my old Dad,
"Please Lord can I have the first dream back, I promise I won't be bad"...

Photo: Manager Darrell Clarke

Welcome Back

There's quite a few welcomes to send out, as we return to the League once more,
Let's start with you the supporters, for this club you're its heart and its core,
You've shown us all how clever you all are, as instead of watching the cricket,
You saved your up money and come back, to buy your Rovers season ticket!

And welcome to our Oxford friends, we hope that the roads have been good,
We congratulate you on promotion, you deserved it as you knew you would,
We send you a West Country welcome, and wish you a season of cheer,
Though you'll understand it when we wish though, that you take no points today from here!

And a welcome back to old players, it's so good to see your return,
We salute you and trust your ambition, inside you will continue to burn,
You did us so proud all last season, I hope your summer was restful and long,
And that batteries recharged you have returned, raring to go, fit and strong.

Again we welcome Mr (it should be Sir) Darrell Clarke, congratulations to you and your wife,
Football aside we all wish the both of you, a long and loving happy life,
We're so glad that no team could 'Leed' you astray, and that loyalty above all did win,
Well, you know that here at the Rovers, it's like being back with your own kin.

A welcome now to the new players, who have come here all hoping to shine,
You'll soon see that as long as you're trying, then for the supporters, you'll do just fine,
You have shown your wisdom in choosing, a club that will be at the races,
As we're greeting each challenge with gusto, 'cos this is a club going places.

New players are tomorrow's new heroes, so take heart lads and make us all proud,
Show us that you've come here as winners, and we'll sing your name out long and loud,
You've joined one big family at Rovers, from boardroom to staff and the fans,
We'll back you 100% if you are trying, we'll back you down to the last man.

A welcome of course to our leaders, to Wael and to Steve and the board,
They are building new solid foundations, and on that we are all in accord,
'Rome' wasn't built in a season, and ambition is often best I have found,
When it's tempered with good planning and wisdom, to get us our lovely new ground.

Patience is more prudent that haste now, and we trust you to make us all proud,
And give us a stadium who's acoustics, mean we won't have to all shout so loud!
And welcome and thanks to the clubs staff, every Bernie, Keith, Clare and Jack,
Without you this club would be nothing, so give yourself a pat on the back.

Welcome back now every one of you, a new division and season awaits,
We've a great team all working together, to bring talent and skill to steer fate,
It's a challenge for sure but one we will meet, as this great club is up for the fight,
Let's make Bristol proud to be Gas once again, as we sing out 'Irene Goodnight'.

The first game back in good old League One!

The Ups and Downs of Football

It's Bolton that we entertain on this typical August night,
And we welcome here the Wanderers, while the evenings are still light,
We hope the journey from the North, has been easy to the Mem,
Though they'll understand it when we hope, they go back pointless once again!

They've had a few tough years it seems, and for them that can't be nice,
It's the supporters I feel sorry for, it's the fans that pay the price,
They tasted life at the very top, and they're fall was no cause for jest,
It's a sombre lesson to all of us, and we wish them all the best.
(The exception being when they play us of course!)

Football's fortunes can be fickle, and they join a growing band,
Where ambition and reality, don't always work out hand in hand,
Take Newcastle and The Villa, who for the first time in many years,
Find themselves out of the top flight, leaving many of their fans in tears.

Look down to the lower leagues, and you'll see some shadows of the past,
Proud names once knowing better times, who thought their time would always last,
Grimsby Town and Stockport, and Hereford to name but a few,
Who once would steal the headlines, but who's sad demise they now rue.

And now we see less glamorous teams, climbing up the table,
Who would have thought that Burton Albion, and Aston Villa would be able,
To play each other in the league, well, it can't help but make one smile,
How the world of football has no set rules, and changes along each mile.

The modern game has no sentiment, and talk of heritage can be funny,
Being called a 'big team' is a fallacy, if you no longer have the money,
A big fan base can mean nothing too, and Portsmouth will confirm that's true,
They have bigger gates than many teams, yet languish in League Two.

It's not a new phenomenon, for the fortunes of clubs to change,
Just look up old league tables, and you'll see how things can rearrange,
No one has the right to demand, to be successful and stay on top,
And as poor Bolton will now testify, it's easy for one's fortunes to drop.

So where are we on this seesaw, as we ponder what might yet be?
Well our fortunes are plainly on the rise, and that's clear for all to see,
And what a story it will make, if we can do well again this year,
From Conference to well, let's just see... On that thought I'll have a beer!

Oh My, England

England oh my England, how I long to see you win,
But your performance against Iceland, was sadly verging on a sin,
I watched in blinking disbelief, as the best that we could muster,
Was to run around in circles, looking lost in clueless bluster.

I try to see the best in you, and think how hard that it might be,
To tear yourself from your summer hols, to play for your own Country,
And I understand how embarrassing, and tough that it must be,
To play under a manager, that had a past link to the City!

Even though I still have my own teeth, I am getting on a bit,
So I'm gladly, or sadly, old enough to recall when England were a hit,
World Cup Willy was on song, and Alf Ramsey made England play,
Good enough to beat everyone, and win the Jules Rimet.

1966 it was and of course, I was just a tot,
And sat around our black and white TV, there was a blooming lot,
Half the street were in our house, 'cos our Dad had a eighteen inch!
Impressive by the standards then, and far too heavy to be pinched!

Pickles was the hero dog, who found the stolen gold World Cup,
He piddled on a little bush, sniffed, then dug the Cup right up!
His owner tried to clean it up, then handed it straight in,
And apart from a faint smell of doggy wee, you wouldn't know where it had been!

Of course the match is famous now, and even the youngest know the score,
Old West Germany pinching two, and England smashing four,
Rule Britannia ruled the waves, and ruled this mighty game,
But sadly fifty years have passed, and it's never been the same.

Since then we've never reached the heights, that we did in 66',
Managers have come and gone, and many average teams been picked,
When you look around for England's best, you might need to take a trip,
Out of the global Premier League, to the English Championship!

One of my proudest recent times, and the one I like a lot,
Was watching our own Rickie Lambert, score against the Scots.
A handful of Rovers legends, have graced both the Gas and England's team,
And the day a current Rover puts on an England shirt... it will fulfil another dream.

Written after Iceland had knocked us out…

Photo: Bristol Rovers' owner Wael Al-Qadi

The Big FA Dinner..

T'was the night of the big FA dinner, the wise and the good were all there,
The champers was flowing like water, and the lamb had, of course, been served rare,
The awards and the prizes were given, and the night was all running to plan,
When a wag who'd had too many sherbets, said "isn't there a prize for the fans?"

The question then caused a commotion, as they realised the fans didn't count,
So they sent out to find a spare trophy, all in gold with a bright shiny mount,
"We've found one" they cried out in triumph, "it's a bit bent but we'll give it a shine,
"We just need to sort out a winner, and everything then will be fine".

Alex Ferguson stood up and ordered, that he knew who had the best fans,
Of course it was (yawn) Man United, all loyal down to the last man,
The great and the good all did listen, and one or two muttered in awe,
But they looked up the rules and declared that for once, Ferguson's word wasn't law!

Abramovich rose to his feet and declared, that just because he was so wealthy,
All the best fans in England just had of course, to be from London's posh Chelsea.
The West Ham chairman argued the case, that The Hammers were now to be bound,
To have the best fans in all of the land, as they had the most subsidised ground!

The Liverpool chairman then had his say, and Man City too made a pitch,
They all seemed to be basing their cases though, on who was the biggest and rich,
The assembling crowd all listened in and pondered what they had all heard,
Just as the puddings arrived yes you've guessed, t'was rich toasted hot lemon curd!

Newcastle waded in proudly, boasting that their fans were all very loyal,
Then Villa did throw in their hat, claiming that one of their fans was a Royal!
Greg Dyke listened hard to all of their shouts, but declared that he just wasn't sure,
Did anyone else still have a claim? He would listen to only one more.

Our Wael then calmly rose to his feet, and the assembly all hushed listening in,
As he told them the tale of our Rovers, and how outstanding the fans all had been,
He lamented of life in The Conference, and how 40,000 had willed them to win,
And the room was plunged into silence, you could have heard the drop of a pin.

Wael told them again of our long troubling years, and how life had rarely been pretty,
Under the shadow of our Red Robin rivals, on the other side of the city,
As he ended he found himself singing, and with emotion the room all joined in,
And as 'Irene Goodnight' filled the rafters, Greg declared that the Gas HAD to win!

He's One of Our Own

When he left his last club, there must have been a 'Vale' of tears,
Returning to us like a long lost son, welcomed home after too many years,
Our club was at its lowest ebb, lost in a conference far from home,
He's one of our own. He's one of our own. Chris Lines, he's one of our own.

As he watched his home team fall from grace, he pondered at our plight,
And in his heart knew that if called, he'd be there to join the fight,
So the decision didn't take very long, when DC asked him here on loan,
He's one of our own. He's one of our own. Oh Darrell, get Chris on the phone.

It takes a very special man, to play beneath where he knew he could,
He could have played way way above, as they all thought that he should,
But he saw our plight and when he heard the call, the seeds were already sown,
He's one of our own. He's one of our own. Chris Lines, he's one of our own.

My pal at Sheffield Wednesday still thinks that they were mad,
And the day that Chrissy left them, was a day they still think bad,
His skills were plain for all to see, and he was never heard to moan,
He's one of our own. He's one of our own. Chris Lines, he's Gas to the bone.

He gave up playing big name teams, to join our survival fight,
And helped take us through The Conference, giving our midfield skill and bite,
His play off goal against Forest Green, was of a quality that stood alone,
He's one of our own. He's one of our own. Oh Chris Lines, he's one of our own.

Never frightened of the big stage, he looks so comfortable on the ball,
Striding through the midfield, and always standing tall,
And when we won at Wembley, you could see how the man had grown,
He's one of our own, he's one of our own, our Chris Lines, he's one of our own.

Then he helped us through League Two, being key to our double top,
Chasing through the midfield, he would run 'til he was fit to drop,
His recent goal against Cardiff, took us to Chelsea and set a new tone,
He's one of our own, yea one of our own, oh Chris Lines, he's one of our own.

When they write up Rovers history, every scholar and Rovers sage,
Will know when they write of 'Linesy', he will need his own special page,
Heroes come in many forms, and this one's a Rover to the bone,
He's one of our own. He's one of our own. Chris Lines, in a class of his own.

On a Serious (English Bank) Note

What is it that we need to have, yet we all try to deny,
Can make a timid woman fight, but yet make a grown man cry,
Will drive us on to do the greatest things, yet bring demons to our fears,
Can make us scream with happiness, but more often bring sad tears.

We none can live without it, and it's a basic fact of life,
That it can bring the most ugly man, the most attractive wife,
It's said to make the world go round, but without it life's not funny,
I am of course referring to, the enigma that is money.

The football world is not exempt, from its blessing and its curse,
In the wrong hands we have all seen, how it can make matters worse,
When used with wisdom it can be, a thing of blessed wonder,
But in the wrong hands it can bring about, despair and darkest thunder.

I was thinking just the other day, that it might be rather nice,
To be rewarded oh so handsomely, like England's Sam Allardyce,
Three mill a year should see most of us, happy and secure,
Yet the demon that is money, drove him to want some more.

We do not know the ins and outs, but what was said seems true,
So yet again our beautiful game has been battered black and blue,
The selfish and the greedy, take money from (ultimately) you and me,
And our great game's dirty washing, is aired for the world to see.

But before we just blame football, we need to comprehend,
That greed is not just in our game, it's all around us in the end,
We've had the banking scandal, and a dozen others too,
Greed it seems is commonplace, and affects both me and you.

It's a sad fact of humanity, that our most basic human drive,
Is to compete and be successful, it's what keeps our brains alive,
Most of us know when to stop, and won't break life's moral code,
But sadly there are a few it seems, that will walk a darker road.

It makes me really angry, that our beautiful game's been seeded,
With parasites and hangers on, that now need to be weeded,
It's morally wrong when Rolls Royces, bring players agents to a ground,
While fathers struggle to bring their kids, and have to look for every pound.

So who's next as England Manager? Who will lead England from the dark?
All is know is that they cannot have... Rovers Darrell Clarke!

It's Time for a Moan

There's a man I see almost every match, for he will rarely miss a game,
And every time without exception, it's always the same same same,
No matter what the subject is, he's like a dog with a very old bone,
He's a champion in his field for sure, which is to moan and moan and moan.

I'd like to teach the world to sing, (in perfect harmony)!
But this chap simply cannot see, the wood for one very large tree,
Some always see their glass half full, and greet the world with smiles,
But this guy's glass is so empty that, I wonder if he's suffering with piles!

Standing at locked turnstiles, he'll watch the seconds slipping by,
And the moment the gates should have opened, out comes his noisy cry,
"Oi, why aren't these gates open, you're late every bloody time,"
Tapping his watch with his finger, like there's been a major crime.
(He has got a point actually; they never are opened on time!)

He called over an official, in the bar only just last week,
To make a serious complaint, and he wasn't being nice or meek,
The subject of his rancour, was that his beer mat had got stuck,
The official smiled politely, but didn't really give a... monkeys!

I'm sure he's getting louder, and his moaning's worse for sure,
Perhaps he should see a Dr (but not me please), but I doubt there is a cure,
I wonder if he's married, and if his wife's the boss at home?
There surely has to be a reason, why he should moan and moan and moan.

And please don't mention referees, for I don't think I could stand,
To hear him shout of Specsavers again, with his usual ferocious demand,
And linesmen they must know him, for they really don't seem to mind,
Him questioning their parentage, or suggesting that they are blind.

If he suffered from depression, that would be a different thing,
He would need our every sympathy, and some help then we would bring,
But it's more habit than is medical, as he moans from inside his pit,
Sadly he can't help it, he's just a miserable ...!
(I do have a rhyme but there might be children listening!)

I'm sure that hidden deep beneath, there might lurk a lovely chap,
One whose positive demeanour, is really to smile and laugh and clap,
So if you know this gentleman, for he will stand out like a mile,
Don't pass him on the other side, but give him your biggest smile!

If you meet someone today who hasn't got a smile, then give them yours.
And in a small way, the world will at least for one person, be a better place...

The Magic Boots

I went down to the old Sunday market, hunting a bargain or two,
When I saw a strange glow in the distance, shimmering in white, then in blue,
The glowing then stopped as I walked up, to a stall that I'd not seen before,
A strange man with a beard and an eye patch, at a stall with one item, no more.

Two football boots were displayed there, the last of their kind then it seems,
"These magical boots are so special, that the wearer will play out their dreams,"
The old man continued by asking, who it was that I watched every match,
So I told him the Pirates of Bristol, and he grinned through his beard and his patch.

"These boots have magical powers, and they'll never grow old or get holes,
But 'tis the boots that will choose the right owner, then that man will always score goals,"
I didn't believe what he said though, but humoured his kindly old way,
And thinking of someone they might fit though, I asked him how much I should pay.

"Just give me your old season ticket", not the one that you're using this year,
And if you see me stood in the club bar, then I'll let you buy me a beer"
I handed my old ticket over, and as he gave me the boots it felt weird,
And ten paces away when I looked back, the man and the stall... disappeared!

The boots didn't fit my young nephew, or anyone else that then tried,
To the point that I then started wondering, if the old man had just simply lied,
Every foot that they tried didn't fit them, and at one point I thought I might scream,
Then I gave them to our Matty Taylor, who declared... that they fit like a dream!

So the magical boots found the right feet, and our Matty then started to rave,
As he found that with his special boots on, no keeper could parry or save,
His shooting and heading were lethal, 'twas like his new boots had found him by fate,
And he shot to the top scoring table, ended the year with a record twenty eight!

Then the strangest of dreams came to Matty, as he laid fast asleep in the sack,
He dreamt that a ghostly old Pirate, had beckoned his boots to come back,
He woke up next day to discover, that his boots were nowhere to be found,
So he put out a sign saying 'Reward', and offered a few hard earned pounds.

With his boots now gone Matty was worried, that without them he might never score,
But then he cracked in a thunderous belter, and then stared scoring some more,
It seemed that the boots were not magic at all, as he rose to match football's elite,
And that all along the magic it seemed, was always in... Matty's feet!

Up the Gas!

Photo: Bristol Rovers Matchday Programme, 'The Pirate'

Read All About It

Watching football was rather different, way back in 1920,
The fans wore bowler hats and ties, and moustaches there were plenty,
(Mainly worn by men in those days)
Rovers played at Eastville then, besides the old gasworks,
And hot Bovril and a cold meat pie, were the only matchday perks.

The Pirate magazine then first appeared, of thin paper it was made,
Just a few scant pages in black and white, with little detail I'm afraid,
The teamsheet gave our players names, and against whom we were playing,
But spoke little of our own dear club, for then no one was really saying.

How different things are now today, with your Pirate magazine,
A programme made for everyone, who's hungry for the Rovers scene,
Over eighty pages bursting full, of interest, facts and fun,
There's something there for everyone, to read come rain or sun.

From the hallowed words of Darrell Clarke, to Lance Cook with Pirate Sounds,
Keith Brookman's literary masterpiece, is a bargain at just three pounds,
Ian Holtby and Ken Masters, update us all with all the news,
While Helpline's Martyn Radnedge, always looks for new True Blues.

Sue Chappell rubs in some Deep Heat, while Ryan Davis has a view,
Stephen Byrne is surely Classic Gas, while Rick Johansen's Eclectic Blue,
Ruth Williams is one proud Rover, as Beth Cole takes a look inside,
And Paul and Dave unveil our brightest lads, to fill us all with pride.

Ian Brommage talks to the younger Gas, as Paul Matz goes back in time,
Jamie Howarth loves old programmes, even though he's in his prime,
Kevin Cook writes of football films, while Graham Mills spies the opposition,
And Steve Smith talks authoritatively, so is often on a mission.

Antony Addy makes a talking point, while Chris Wathen gives some thought,
Now I'll bet you hadn't realised, just how much your three pounds bought?
On Mark Leesdad's Double Bubble, no one could ever pass,
While Nathan Bees will alway say, that life is just a Gas. (And he's right)

Roy Cowell commends the Presidents club, while Peter Gibson's looking home,
And Mike Jay and Stephen Byrne's club data, is in a class all of its own,
On and on the pages flow, all designed by our Ann Walter,
Then Keith Brookman adds a page or ten, that no one needs to alter.

Pensord printers race to press, with its cover shouting loud,
And the resulting matchday programme, should make Gasheads feel so proud,
There's something there for everyone, and it won't make your wallet bleed,
And the only thing that I have to say, is that it takes so long to read!

We Be Bristle Kiddies...
(With apologies to Non Bristolians)

Ow biss den my babee, ware de biss den kid?
Bet ewe bin down to da Mem, wiv me ole Dad Sid,
Av deece bin wiv day Gas-eds, avin a good time,
See dee for a pinta scrump? Well deece wont be drinkin wine!

I bin watchin Bristle Rovers, iss slike I'm sat dare wiv me kin,
Wuz luvly seein all day Gas-eds, av anudder win,
Me bellee started rumblin, see I ad'nt et a lot,
So I ad a gurt big pastee, an it shore did it da spot.

If eye stays a day away now, I comes back in a rush,
Cuz eye wuz brung up ear in Bristle, an I eye finks it is gurt lush,
From St. Anns upta Orefield, eye finks iss bloomin grate,
De only place I don't like, is down durr at Trashton Gate.

I drove up to da Smoke lass week, it leff eye feelin cauld,
All day carz an traffik dare, made I feel quite auld,
I ate id all day citee types, wiv all dare lar-de-dar,
I giv it up insida our, an jump back in me car.

I cum tearin down da M4, an ida joined a gurt big queue,
Az longaz at da end of it, I cud see da M-firty-too,
I luves it ear my babbee, ida pass on all day rest,
Cuz az dat Tina Turner sez, it simply izda best!

Day says our accents dyin owt, but it ain't ear ware iss blue,
Are Bristle accents live n well, my ears tell I dat is true,
Ah sure, dares lots of uvers ear, like Poles n all alike,
But even day is learning how, to speak Bristle clear an right.

I ear dem avin lessons, from neyburs an new frends,
Dale drop they funny accents soon, an talk proper in da end,
All eye nose is watt eye ear, an dat iz Bristle's doin well,
But watt worries eye is dat they uvers, juss don't no owta spell!

Toodle Pip! Up the Gas!

The Magic of the Cup...

I can feel the tension mounting, as its once again that time,
I confess I'd hoped not to be here, so now I need to find a rhyme!
Brave Crawley battled very hard, determined to have their say,
Forcing us on this cold Tuesday night, to an exciting Cup replay.

There's something about the FA Cup, it's unique in every way,
Which is why we have all turned out now, on this dark November day,
The second round is calling, does a clash with Taunton await?
Wouldn't that be great for the West, a tie conjured up by fate.

My heart had started pounding, when the draw was being made,
The BBC had staged the set, and of no one was I afraid,
And all around the country, nerves were frayed and raw,
Fingers crossed for ball 32, lets hope for a decent draw...

Our hopes are born and captured, inside this cup of dreams,
The minnow and the big boys, still eleven men in each team,
Passion makes new heroes, and each year a few new ones come,
Dreaming of the third round, with the big boys in the drum.

But back now to the game tonight, and a tricky match in sight,
Crawley Town have quality, and seem right up for the fight,
It's good to see Matt Harrold back, as he always gave his best,
But let's hope that our boys in blue, will win through tonight's test.

But... What's in a Cup?

Whilst the FA Cup has great magic, I must say I'm afraid,
I can't say I hold such feelings, for the 'Checkatrade',
Hijacked by the big teams, to give their kids a game,
The 'Leyland Daf' (and its later names), has never been the same.

Who ever dreamt up the 'Checkatrade', needs to think again,
The fans have shown their feelings, and treat it with distain,
Not ever has there been a cup, so contrived and ill thought out,
Which is why most of you stayed at home, because it wasn't worth a shout!

Come on Ref!

Are you sitting comfortably? Then my tale I will begin,
It's the story of a football team, that always tried to win,
They worked so very very hard, but sometimes couldn't see,
That they could beat almost every team, but not... the referee.

They passed the ball so very fast, and it gave their fans such pride,
Though their speed so often sadly meant, that they were wrongly judged offside,
The linesmen simply could not see, that when the ball was played,
That Ellis or Matt were just ONSIDE, but the ref would not be swayed.

And linesmen also seemed to have, a downer on this team,
They seemed to miss the obvious foul, as if out there in a dream,
They'd only flag for offsides, or if the ball went out of play,
And ignore a stonewall penalty, like they didn't like to say.

So when we scored they'd hesitate, and look to the ref to check,
If some late decision might, turn a great goal to a wreck,
Only when the whistle went, would they start to celebrate,
Which is why their celebrations, were often muted and quite late.

We've all seen refs magnificent, who referee without a care,
The game flows oh so very well, one would hardly know they're there,
It's a pleasure watching with them, and they make a good game great,
It's the ones with lesser qualities though, who just make us all irate!

But...

I remember when I was fit and young, that I refereed a game,
Then I found that with the whistle, it just wasn't at all the same,
I thought it would be easy, with my red and yellow card,
But found it very difficult, and really rather hard.

The players started shouting, and asking me to find,
A stronger pair of glasses, and said I must be blind,
I ran around like I see them do, wishing I was deaf,
But it made me then appreciate - how hard it is to ref.

So as I sit here in my comfy stand, gazing down on the play,
Exasperated by some decisions, not going our deserved way,
Then I remember my experience, so don't condone that nasty song,
For referees are just like all of us, it's so easy to get it wrong...
(Still get blooming frustrated though. Ask Daniel Leadbitter!)

Christmas is Coming...

Christmas is coming and the Goose is getting fat,
So it's time again to dust off, your Rovers Christmas hat,
The radio's full of Christmas songs, getting an annual play,
And let's hope we get an early gift, with three points again today.

A warm welcome to Bury, it's always good to see them here,
We suggest they try our pasties, with a pint of Christmas cheer,
It's quite a journey down to here, so we hope the roads were kind,
But we'd rather like to win today, and hope that they don't mind.

Time to buy the turkey soon, and some festive roasting joints,
And it's time to send my Santa letter, requesting lots of points,
I hope he's feeling generous, and that what I've heard is true,
That beneath his garish red coat, he's wearing white and blue.

I heard that Santa's costume, was dreamt up by Diet Coke,
But looking at his rotund frame, that just has to be a joke,
He might claim anorexia, but I'm really not that naive,
It's a good job that we know he's real, or we simply might not believe!

We'll next be here on Boxing Day, probably full of Christmas pud,
Sober as church door mice of course, just as we know we should,
The presents will be open, and the feasting almost done,
And the footy here on Boxing Day, will probably be more fun.

I've done with buying presents now, done with writing cards,
I've bought the club shop out again, it wasn't all that hard,
My wife requested diamond rings, and a Rolex for her wrist,
She'll get nowt but a Rovers shirt, (so I'll have to get her ... drunk!)

My family's getting Rovers gear, just like they did last year,
It's a shame that in the club shop, they don't sell a Rovers beer,
Coffee mugs and woolly hats, the shop is full of treats,
A Rovers Poem Book for granny, and blue slippers for her feet!

I'm so grateful for the Rovers shop, it's saved my skin once more,
So even my old City friends, look like Gasheads out on tour,
Christmas is coming quickly now, so there's only one thing left to say,
To wish you a Gastastic Christmas, and three points again today!

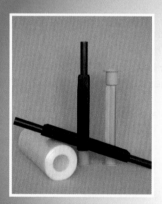

Goodbye to a Special Year

Greetings Gasheads old and young, and welcome here today,
And welcome friends from Wimbledon, down from London way,
You come here on a special day, this the last one of the Year,
And at midnight we shall be welcoming, a new one without fear.

There's rarely been a better time to follow this Rovers team,
Optimism now abounds, that we will soon fulfil our dream,
This year has been a momentous one, in this proud club's history,
And I'm sure I speak for everyone, when I say that I'm liking what I see.

Behind the scene we are witnessing, more than just evolution,
Wael and Steve are quietly bringing about a revolution,
At last we have ambition, and the future's looking bright,
For once in this fair city, the future's blue and white!

And on the pitch we're witnessing, a historic team of men,
Who took us from dark Conference days, back into the light again,
They all play truly for the shirt, and make every Gashead proud,
So the bond between the fans and team, is crystal clear and loud.

In Darrell Clarke we've found a man, with strength and integrity,
That feeds down throughout all the team, then beyond to you and me,
He seems to have the Midas touch, and so many wrongs he has righted,
I'll be watching the New Year's honours list, 'cos I think he should be knighted!

I have a feeling next year, will be as exciting as the last,
And know that 'Rag Bag Rovers', is an image now confined to the past,
This club is changing rapidly, there's something almost every day,
But the important thing really is, that it's being changed in the right way.

Sing 'Auld Lang Syne' and raise a cheer, as the old year slips away,
We wish you all the very best, on this auspicious day,
I hope we end the old year, in a very special way,
Starting out this afternoon, with three more points today!

Happy New Year everyone

Sweet Memories

If you could travel back in time, which game would you watch again?
What moment in Rovers history, what memory for you will remain?
Your age will of course determine, from what era you best recall,
But I bet you've got one special match, which stands out most of all.

Was it back at Chelsea, just a little while ago?
Or last May against Dagenham, well for some that may be so,
Others may hark back to long ago, but there always is a reason,
Why one match stands above all others, some in a special season.

Some can go back to Bert Tann's days, but there's sadly not so many,
While anyone claiming a game before, well, I doubt if there are any,
It's marvellous when you meet old fans, who can recall way back when,
Sparking images in black and white, brought back to life again.

For me I have fond memories, with many matches standing out,
Trips to both Wembley Stadiums, amidst The Pirates' roar and shout,
To be amongst that sea of blue, near forty thou' or more,
Bring proud memories of some special days, when the Gas have gone on Tour.

Outstanding in the memory, is one month in 2007,
When trips to the Millennium AND Wembley, almost took us to Gas heaven,
We won the game we needed to, for promotion was the prize,
And who can forget Sammy's Igoe's run, so big in heart, if not in size.

I've fond memories of old Eastville, and can still feel the sights and sound,
Of hearing the famous Tote End roar, echoing across the ground,
Beating Man United, and winning the Watney Cup,
Spark memories of some grand old times, to cheer any Gashead up.

And the first reign of Gerry Francis, brings sweet memories to the fore,
He built a side to stir the blood, and left us wanting more,
Thumping City at Trumpton, is a memory of the very best,
I could carry that one to my grave, and almost disregard the rest.

But for me my most cherished memory, was at 3.00am one morning,
I'd been asleep but rudely woken, sharp and without warning,
We'd won 3-0 at Blackpool, and being crowned champions was our right,
And in the silence of the night, a lone Gashead sang 'Irene Goodnight'.

To wake up in Blackpool and hear the raw pride in this one lone (and very drunk) Gashead's rendition of 'Irene', cleared the fog of sleep with an immediate thought that yes, we'd won the league! His song breaking the silence of the night brought such a smile to my face that it was worth being woken up for. And I do believe that this current team will achieve even greater things and bring us even greater memories in the years to come...

Oh, Lay Me Down...

When I've gone then burn my bones, and find the centre spot,
Dig a hole and place me there, deep down there in a pot,
I'll then be there for kick offs, and for every Rovers goal,
No one can say that Rovers then, won't play without a soul!

And when we move to a new ground, make sure I'm taken there,
Underneath the centre spot, where I'll rest without a care,
I'll watch the seasons come and go, as winters turn to spring,
And see the grass cut ten thousand times, now that will be a thing.

If we should lose you may hear my sigh, lost gently on the breeze,
But each win will lift my spirits high, and is surely bound to please,
You may think you hear a distant voice, as I sing 'Irene Goodnight',
For my spirit will be singing loud, and my world will be alright.

I'll never feel the cold again, or frown when I forget my hat,
All worldly pain behind me, I'll be bothered by none of that,
I'll make friends with all the pigeons, and will always keep my station,
And do my best to help the groundsman, with his irrigation.

I may float about from time to time, but you'll mistake me for some mist,
You'll rub your eyes and change your drink, thinking you were... Drunk!
It would be great on matchdays, to hear the Gasheads singing,
And feel the joy that Rovers bring, to all when they are winning.

Fear nothing from my presence here, for I'll bring my sense of humour,
You can deny me ever being here, and say it's just a rumour,
But at every local derby game, I shall call on my sense of pity,
By standing at the away end, freaking out the City!

And as long years pass I'll still be here, not troubled then by age,
I'll celebrate every single goal, and read every programme page,
My ghost will linger silently, though some may claim they hear it,
And when we win the Premiership, I'll be singing so loud... In spirit!

Up the Gas!